BOOK ANALYSIS

By Candice Kent

Life and Times of Michael K

BY J. M. COETZEE

J. M. COETZEE

SOUTH AFRICAN-BORN NOVELIST

- **Born in Cape Town in 1940.**
- **Notable works:**
  - *Disgrace* (1999), novel
  - *Summertime* (2009), novel
  - *The Schooldays of Jesus* (2016), novel

John Maxwell Coetzee grew up in Cape Town and completed his Bachelor degree in English and mathematics at the University of Cape Town. He was later a Fulbright scholar at the University of Texas at Austin, where he was awarded a PhD in English. From 1968 to 1971, Coetzee was employed by the State University of New York at Buffalo. In 1971, he returned to South Africa and taught at the University of Cape Town until his retirement in 2002. He subsequently immigrated to Australia and became a citizen of the country in 2006. Coetzee was the first novelist to win the Booker Prize twice, first for *Life and Times of Michael K* (1983) and then for *Disgrace* (1999). He was awarded the Nobel Prize in Literature in 2003.

LIFE AND TIMES OF MICHAEL K

NOVEL

- **Genre:** novel
- **Reference edition:** Coetzee, J. M. (2015) *Life and Times of Michael K*. London: Vintage.
- **1st edition:** 1983
- **Themes:** war, mother-son relationships, South Africa, nature, life

Life and Times of Michael K is set against the backdrop of a fictional civil war in apartheid South Africa. The first chapter is the longest and begins by giving a brief outline of Michael K's early years. Michael's mother, Anna, wishes to return to the farm where she spent her childhood. The pair set off for the Karoo, Anna dies on the way, but Michael continues with her ashes. He finds what he thinks to be the farm and spreads her ashes over a piece of land which he begins to cultivate. His pleasure in this activity is disrupted, but he returns to continue his work on the land, until he is discovered by soldiers who suspect him of supplying the rebels and is sent to a rehabilitation camp. The second, much shorter, chapter is told from the point of view of the medical officer at the camp, who is profoundly affected by Michael's unwillingness to eat. The third and shortest chapter tells of Michael's escape from the camp and his return to his mother's Cape Town dwelling, where he fantasises about journeying back to the farm.

SUMMARY

CAPE TOWN AND THE JOURNEY

The action of the novel begins when Michael is 31. His mother, Anna, has been discharged from a brief but miserable sojourn in hospital. Michael fetches her from hospital and stays on with her in the tiny, musty room that her employers have allocated to her.

It is evident that the country is in a state of disarray. The hospitals and bus service are barely functional and a curfew is in place. Anna wishes to escape the food queues and the violence of the city. She proposes that Michael resign from his job and that they make their way back to the Karoo farm where she grew up.

Michael buys train tickets and tries unsuccessfully to obtain a permit to leave the Cape Town peninsula from the defunct bureaucracy. Whilst the pair waits for their permits, rioting and chaos break out in Sea Point. Michael builds a cart and persuades his mother to allow him to wheel her in the belief that they will get lifts from passing trucks along the way.

The conditions of the journey are harsh. It is cold and wet, no one stops for them, they have to sleep in the bush and they are set upon by thieves. Michael realises that the journey will take much longer than he had expected. Further signs of the country's state of disarray are apparent: there are few vehicles on the road aside from military convoys, and there are many people walking. Anna's health worsens and Michael takes her to a hospital in Stellenbosch, where she dies and is cremated.

Michael is given his mother's ashes. He lingers about Stellenbosch for a while, living as a homeless person and mixing occasionally with vagrants. One day whilst he is walking along a road, a cart stops for him, and hesitating only a moment, K (as he is referred to by the narrator) accepts the offer of a lift. He decides to take his mother's ashes back to where she was born.

K walks for days, sleeping in the bush and eating very little. He is stopped at a road block outside of Worcester and is forced to join an unpaid labour gang. The men are made to clear the railway track which has been buried by rubble displaced by an explosion. K then continues his journey overland, avoiding the roads. When he reaches Prince Albert, he makes enquiries and finds a deserted farmhouse that once belonged to the Visagies.

PRINCE ALBERT AND THE FARM

K spends his days at the farm dam. He clears a patch of land and scatters his mother's ashes. He finds a packet of pumpkin seeds in the shed and begins to cultivate the patch of land. K's days are filled with this work, and he finds a deep pleasure in it. His solitary happiness is interrupted when the Visagies' grandson arrives. Visagie has deserted the army and has come to the farm to hide. He assumes K is a former servant of his grandparents' and expects K to do his bidding.

When Visagie sends him on an errand to Prince Albert, K decides to head for the mountains instead. He lives in a cave and at first scavenges for food, but gradually gives up all effort to live. He sleeps for long periods and finally, when he becomes very sick, creeps down the mountainside and enters the town. He is picked up by the police and placed in a camp for vagrants where the conditions are abysmal. K, like the other men, is forced to work for very low wages. After an attack on Prince Albert by the rebels, the local police take over the camp. Believing the inhabitants to have been involved in the attack, they deny them food.

K climbs the fence and escapes the camp. He returns to the farm. There is no trace of the young Visagie. Nevertheless, K decides to make a hidden shelter for himself near to the dam. He begins to cultivate again, working at night so as to escape detection. One day, from his shelter, he witnesses a group of rebels passing across the land, and is briefly tempted to join them.

K delights in his crop of pumpkins and melons, but soon after they ripen he is discovered by a contingent of soldiers. They suspect him of supplying the rebels and, finding him sickly and weak from semi-starvation, they have him transported to a rehabilitation centre in Cape Town.

INTERNMENT AND ESCAPE

Chapter Two is written in the first person and is considerably shorter than Chapter One. It gives an account of K's time of internment from the point of view of the medical officer at the centre. We never learn the name of the narrator, but unlike the third person narrator of the previous chapter he refers to K as Michaels. He is fascinated by Michaels' unwillingness to eat and by his unworldly personality. He reflects that although Michaels is locked up as an insurgent, he is barely aware that there is a war on. The medical officer makes every effort to persuade his superior, Major Noël van Rensburg, that Michaels is innocent. He tries to get Michaels to speak and to tell his story in order to protect him from the Prince Albert police, who wish to interrogate him over the recent attack on the town's water supply. In the end the narrator and the Major make up a story for the police. Michaels refuses to be fed by tube and the medical officer attempts to feed him butternut squash. The medical officer is profoundly affected by Michaels and writes a letter in which he addresses Michaels urging him to eat. When he discovers that Michaels has escaped, he imagines himself following after him.

Chapter Three returns to the third person narrator, and the protagonist is again referred to only as K. This chapter is very brief. K returns to Sea Point. He is befriended by vagrants, a man and two women he claims are his sisters. They are charitable to him, but also attempt to rob him when he is inebriated by the drink they offer him. When they leave him alone, he makes his way back to his mother's old dwelling place, the room under the staircase in a block of flats, where he fantasises about returning to the farm.

CHARACTER STUDY

MICHAEL K

In the first sentence of the novel we learn that the main character, Michael K, is born in Cape Town with a hare lip. He is taken out of school at an early stage because of his disfigured appearance and because he is considered to be mentally impaired. He is placed in a state home called Huis Norenius, where the children are always hungry.

At 15, K leaves the home and becomes a municipal gardener. Michael is happiest when he is on his own and he dislikes physical intimacy. Michael has come to the conclusion that he exists to look after his mother. When she expresses the wish to return to the home of her youth, on a farm in the Karoo where her parents worked as labourers, Michael makes plans to convey her there. She dies en route, but Michael continues on the journey, taking her ashes with him. He spreads the ashes on a farm, which he believes may have been her childhood home.

Finding the farmhouse abandoned, Michael sleeps in the house but feels uncomfortable there. He kills a feral goat to eat but finds the experience so distressing that he decides instead to live off birds and plants. Michael derives his greatest pleasure from cultivating the seeds he finds in the farm shed. He thinks of the seedlings as his children. He works hard and eats almost nothing. His peace is broken, however, by the arrival of a young man, an army deserter and grandson to the farm owners. Distressed by the loss of his solitude and freedom, Michael leaves and dwells in the mountains until, sick and starved, he descends into the town, where he is incarcerated in a camp along with other vagrants. The men are forced to work for minimal wages and Michael gives half his wages to his friend, Robert, who has a family to support.

When the opportunity arises, Michael escapes and returns to the farm, where he finds fulfilment again in the cultivation of the land, though he continues to exist in semi-starvation. He is discovered by soldiers and detained on the suspicion that he is supplying the rebels. Once again, Michael is incarcerated, this time in a rehabilitation camp in Cape Town, where he refuses to eat or to be fed by tubes. Michael escapes this camp too and returns to the room his mother occupied as a domestic servant, where he fantasises about journeying back to the farm.

Although Michael is perceived as a simpleton by many of the people he interacts with, his thoughts as they are presented by the third person omniscient narrator reveal him to be capable of original and profound reflection.

ANNA K

Michael's mother Anna K suffers from dropsy, a disease which causes the swelling of legs, arms and belly to the point at which she is unable to walk and barely able to breathe. She spends a period in hospital, during which she is neglected, sexually harassed and witnesses the intense suffering and deaths of other patients. She weeps when she sees her son, hiding her tears from all the others. In spite of her condition, Anna is denied a wheelchair by the hospital and it takes hours to get home on a bus service which is clearly disintegrating.

Anna's life has been a harsh one. When Michael is born Anna is repelled by her baby's hare lip and keeps him away from other children because she is offended by their smiles and comments. He is her fourth child, her third child has died, and the first two children have forgotten her.

Anna has been working for the past eight years as a domestic servant. Her employers, the Buhrmanns, live in a five-roomed flat in Sea Point overlooking the Atlantic. Anna has been allocated a storage room under the stairs as her living quarters. The room is unsafe and has no electric lights or ventilation. When the dropsy sets in, she is no longer able to do the cleaning work, but the Buhrmanns keep her on to do the cooking. She lives in fear of the day when their charity will end, and dreams of returning to the quiet Karoo district of her girlhood, where her father had been a farm labourer.

THE MEDICAL OFFICER

The unnamed first person narrator of Chapter Two is a pharmacist by training who has become the medical officer of a rehabilitation and internment camp. He has a close relationship with the

Major in charge of the internment centre, whom he usually refers to by his first name, Noël. The Major has come out of retirement to run the camp and, along with the medical officer, attempts to run the camp as humanely as possible. The medical officer seeks to understand Michael and concludes that the garden Michael seeks is a metaphor for a place in which Michael does not feel homeless.

ANALYSIS

NARRATION

When an author tells a story, he or she has to select a point of view from which the account of events and descriptions of characters is given. This is referred to as the narrative mode of the fictional work and is one of the key factors to consider in the analysis of a novel. The most commonly used modes of narration are third person and first person narratives.

Coetzee uses a third person narrator to tell Michael K's story in Chapter One and Chapter Three. This type of narrator is outside the story. According to convention, an omniscient third person narrator possesses all the necessary knowledge about the events of the novel. A third person narrator may also be intrusive if he or she is not restricted to mere reporting, but guides us in our evaluation of the characters' motives, their perspectives on life and their personal qualities. However, the narrator of *Life and Times of Michael K* is unobtrusive, or impersonal, and tends to only present the action in dramatic scenes without any commentary or judgement. Such a narrator is considered to be objective.

The objectivity of Coetzee's third person narrator in this novel is further enhanced by his or her limited point of view, which is restricted to the perceptions, memories, thoughts and feelings of the protagonist, Michael K, and to a lesser extent of Anna K. In this respect, the narrator of *Life and Times of Michael K* differs from a third person omniscient narrator, who is also privy to the mental and emotional processes of all the other characters.

Coetzee departs from third person narration in Chapter Two, where he adopts a first person narrative perspective. The narrative 'I' of Chapter Two is the unnamed medical officer of the rehabilitation camp. Unlike the third person narrator, the first person narrator is therefore a participant, albeit a peripheral one, in Michael K's story. The material of the first person narrator's story is naturally limited to his knowledge, understanding, experience and inferences.

CONTEXT: APARTHEID

Life and Times of Michael K was published in 1983 during the apartheid era in South Africa. Apartheid was a policy of separate development based on white supremacist notions. The system was initiated in 1948 and began to be dismantled in the 1990s. As early as 1913, the Natives Land Act allocated 90 percent of the land in the country to white people, even though they comprised a mere 20 percent of the population. The remaining 10 percent of the land was allocated to the majority black population. Farms, like the Visagie farm, which Michael K occupies, would have therefore belonged only to white people. In 1923, the Urban Areas Act was passed to enforce residential segregation. The National Party came into power in 1948 and the state began to pass numerous pieces of discriminatory legislation. People were classified according to race and this was registered in identity documents. Every adult black person was required to carry a pass book indicating whether he or she had permission to be in a particular region. Interracial marriages were banned and even sex between people of different races was forbidden. The Prevention of Illegal Squatting Act

(1951) allowed for the forced removal of those living in informal settlements. These and many other oppressive laws were brutally enforced by the apartheid regime. As a consequence of the political system, the black population was relegated to servant roles, remaining impoverished and therefore separated by a great wealth divide from the privileged white population. Coetzee's novel makes no direct reference to race. The reader is left to infer such detail from the context of the period.

This state of affairs was not passively accepted by the black majority. The African National Congress (ANC), which had existed in an earlier form with the goal of achieving voting rights for non-whites, opposed apartheid. After protests in Sharpville against the pass laws led to the massacre of 69 people, the ANC was banned in 1960. Although initially dedicated to non-violent means, the movement established a military wing, which employed guerrilla tactics against the apartheid structure.

THEME: WAR

The backdrop to Michael K's story is a fictional civil war in South Africa. The first reference to the state of war is made in passing, a couple of pages into the novel when Anna reflects on her hospital experience. She fears the indifference that she will meet with as an elderly woman with an ugly affliction in a society preoccupied with and made anarchic by war.

Whilst the war occupies the minds and lives of his fellow men and women, Michael lives in an alternate time, in a state of bliss cultivating his patch of land on the Visagies' farm. The war slips out of his mind and he manages to live apart from it, only occasionally reminded of its existence when he hears jet fighters overhead.

The war, however, intrudes when Michael's peace and solitude is disrupted by the young Visagie, who has deserted the army and has come to hide from the military police on the farm. Visagie tells Michael that many men are deserting the army, and that the war will soon be over. The implication is that the guerrillas will win. In his discussion with Michael, the guard at the Prince Albert labour camp shows a similar disinclination to commit to the war. Although, as Michael reflects, the guerrillas are reported by radio to have been killed in great numbers, Visagie's conviction that the state will be defeated by the rebels in the near future is echoed in Chapter Two in the medical officer's discussions with the Major. Both men anticipate the day when the guerrilla forces will enter the rehabilitation camp.

With the exception of Noël's observation about the purpose of the war being to ensure that minorities have a say in their destinies, there is no political commentary or explanation of the war. However, Michael is tempted to follow the rebels when he spots them crossing the farm. He does not feel the same repulsion for these young men, who he knows blow up railway lines, mine roads and attack farmhouses, as he feels for the soldiers and for the police. He resists the temptation, however, because he believes that there must be men who remain behind and continue to garden.

FURTHER REFLECTION

SOME QUESTIONS TO THINK ABOUT...

- Which narrative methods does Coetzee employ?
- What effects does the author achieve with different methods of narration, and what are their respective strengths and limitations?
- What do you think gives this novel its universal appeal?
- Explore the character of Michael K by reflecting on what motivates him.
- How does Coetzee deal with the theme of war?
- How does the novel depict the relationship between mother and son?
- What is the political and social context of this novel?
- What references, explicit and implicit, does the novel make to the social and political context of apartheid South Africa?

We want to hear from you!
Leave a comment on your online library
and share your favourite books on social media!

FURTHER READING

REFERENCE EDITION

- Coetzee, J. M. (2015) *Life and Times of Michael K*. London: Vintage.

REFERENCE STUDIES

- Abrams, M. H. (1999) *A Glossary of Literary Terms*. Fort Worth: Harcourt Brace.

MORE FROM BRIGHTSUMMARIES.COM

- Reading guide – *Waiting for the Barbarians* by J. M. Coetzee.

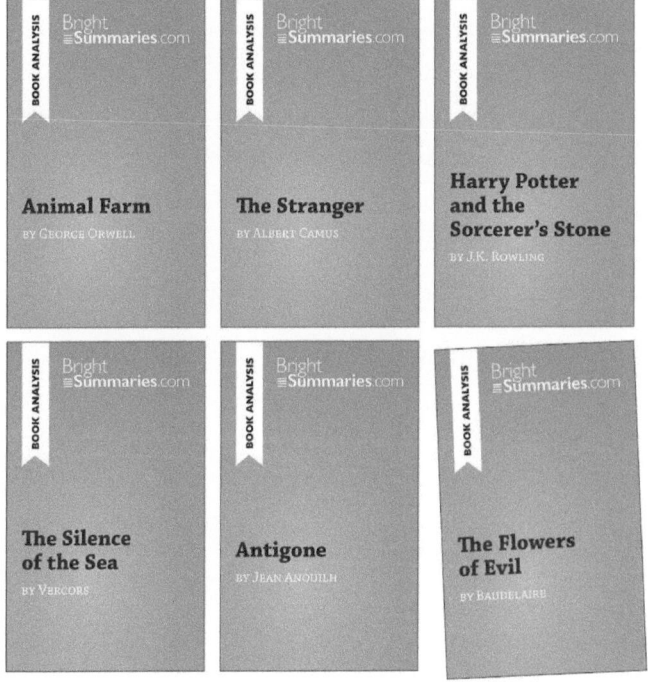

Although the editor makes every effort to verify the accuracy of the information published, BrightSummaries.com accepts no responsibility for the content of this book.

www.brightsummaries.com

Ebook EAN: 9782808015806

Paperback EAN: 9782808015813

Legal Deposit: D/2018/12603/549

Cover: © Primento

Digital conception by Primento, the digital partner of publishers.